TOLMAN LOSEY

What's In
A Leg?

To Jonathan, who first asked the question,
and to children everywhere who want to know

Copyright © 1987 by Janice Schwegler
Published by Price/Stern/Sloan Publishers, Inc.
360 North La Cienega Boulevard, Los Angeles, California 90048

ISBN 0-8431-1980-2

What's In
A Leg?

by
Janice
Schwegler

PRICE/STERN/SLOAN
Publishers, Inc., Los Angeles

What's in my leg? Would you like to know?
How is it made and what makes it go?

When I think of all I can do with my legs,
I understand better what each part must play.

To hold up my body, my legs must be strong.
Like poles, tall and straight,
　　my legs must have BONE.

Bones are hard on the outside,
  but softer within.
My ankles and knees let my legs bend.

For moving my bones,
    my MUSCLES must act.
A muscle can shorten—
    we say it contracts.

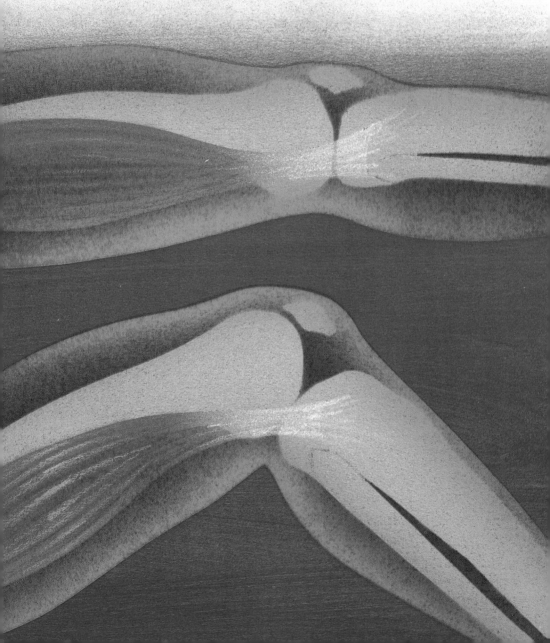

Like a row of toy soldiers
that move closely in
When muscles contract,
the bones move with them.

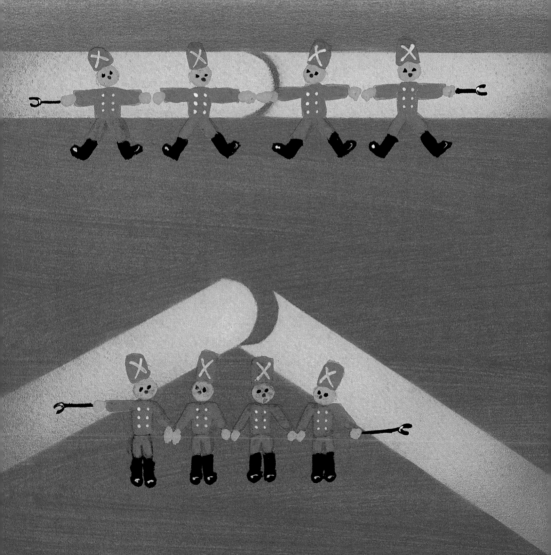

And how does muscle contraction occur?
Like telephone wires,
  each muscle has NERVES.

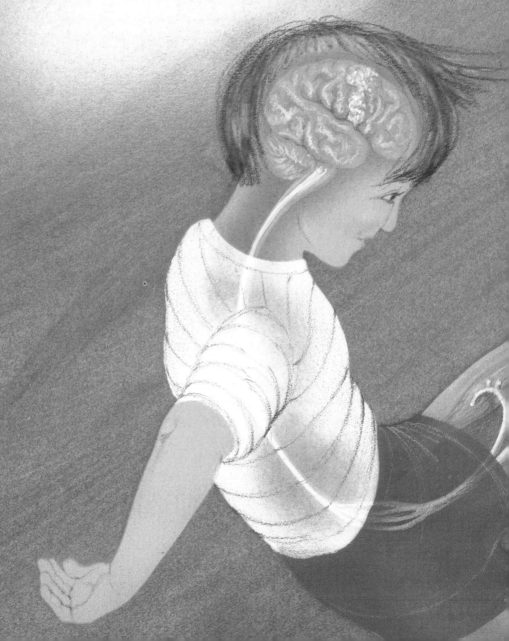

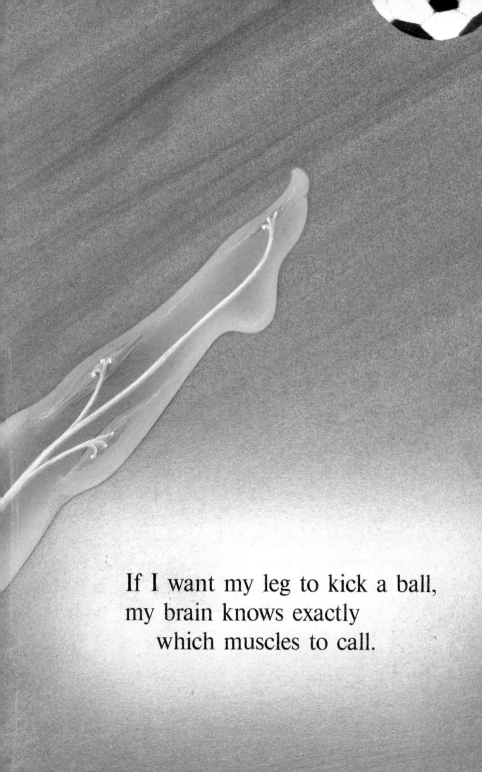

If I want my leg to kick a ball,
my brain knows exactly
which muscles to call.

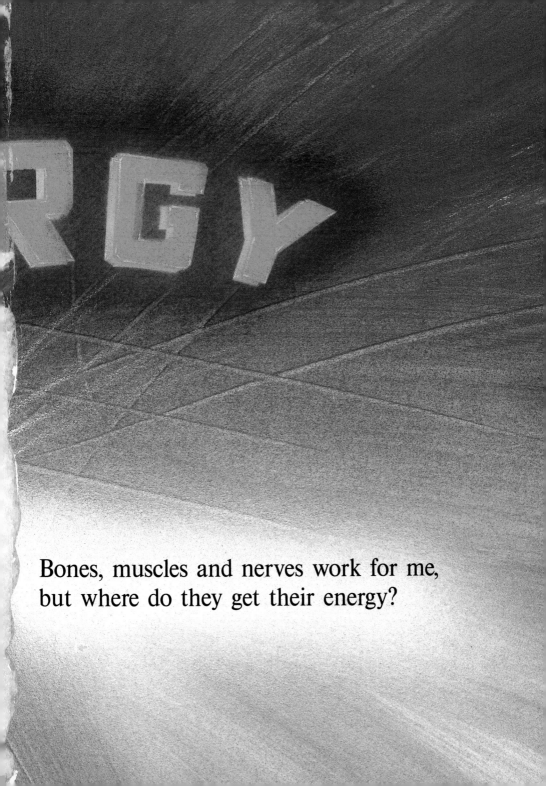

Bones, muscles and nerves work for me,
but where do they get their energy?

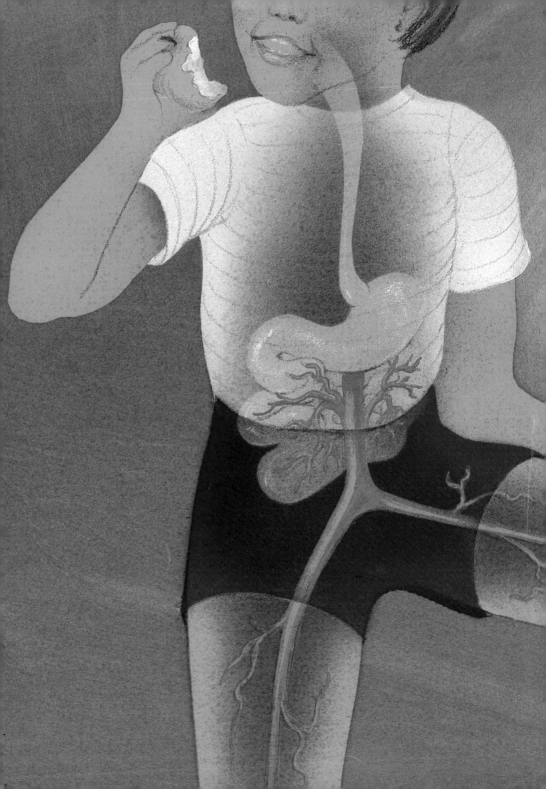

Energy comes in when I eat good food.
Small pieces of food go into my BLOOD.

Blood goes to bones, muscles and nerves,
bringing food-energy to make them work.

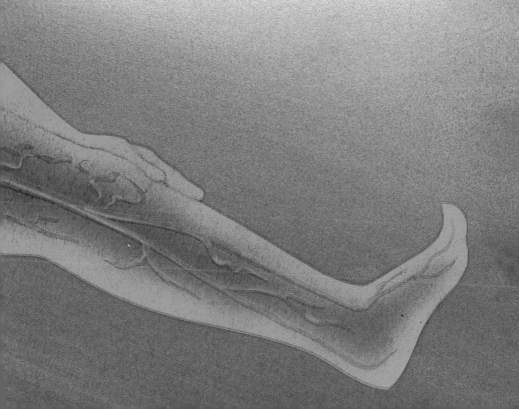

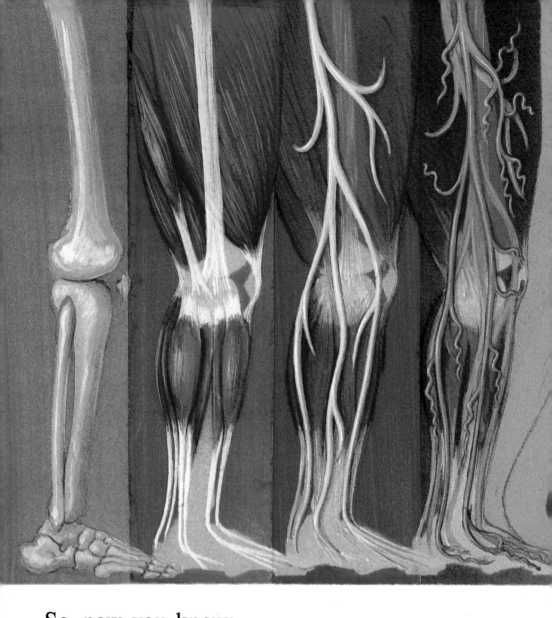

So, now you know:
    BONE makes my legs strong and straight,
    MUSCLES make it move,
    NERVES bring the message,
    BLOOD brings it fuel.

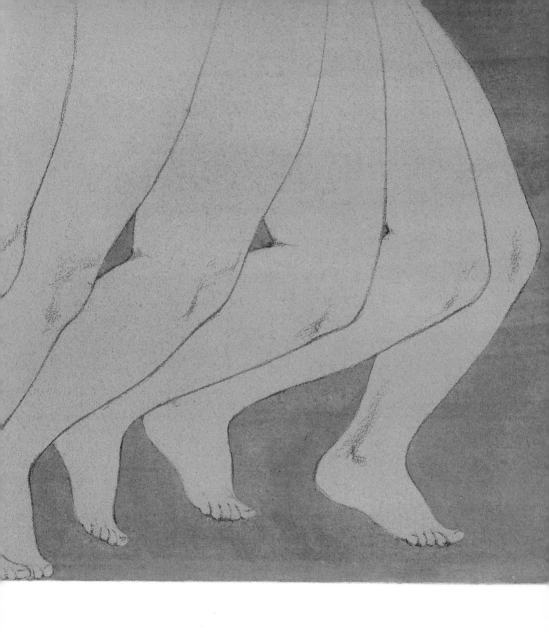

All work together to make my legs go!

But there's still one last part
    that keeps bad things out
    and the good things safely in.
It's what I can see and touch—
    my SKIN.

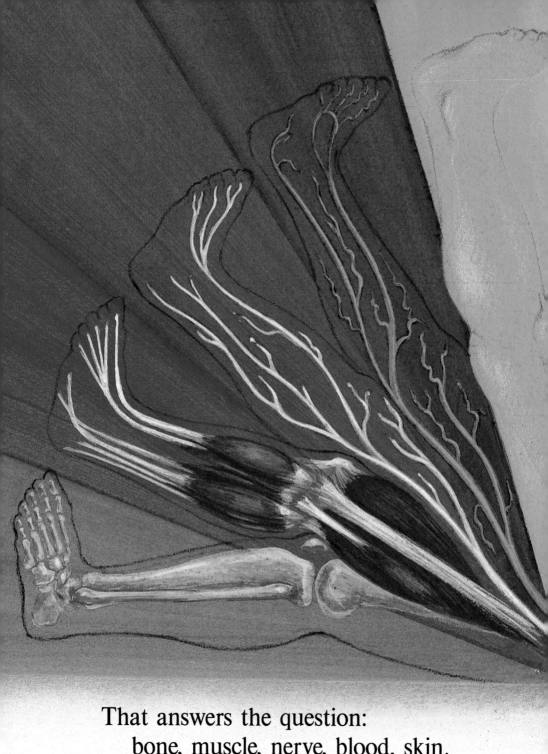

That answers the question:
bone, muscle, nerve, blood, skin.

That's what's in my leg!

So, I eat good food and
take care when I play...

Now that I know what's in my legs!